The Future Scrapbook

Having the Design of Your Life™

Nicholas Hall

RD Whitney & Co.

The Future Scrapbook - Having the Design of Your Life™

Publisher's Cataloging-in-Publication
(Provided by Quality Books, Inc.)

Hall, Nicholas John
    The Future Scrapbook : having the design of your life / Nicholas Hall. -- 1st ed.
      p. cm.
      LCCN : 99-91151
      ISBN : 0-9675189-0-3

      1. Goal (Psychology) 2. Planning. 3.Success -- Psychological aspects. 4. Self-actualization (Psychology) 5. Visualization.   I. Title.

BF505.G6H35 2000   158.1

QBI99-1479

Text and cover design by Creative Connections

First Edition: February 2000

10 9 8 7 6 5 4 3 2 1

Dedication

To my wife, Jennifer, the love of my life, whose unending support is beyond comprehension.

To my Mom and Dad, for providing just the right amount of guidance and freedom, enabling me to be open to all that life has to offer.

Acknowledgment

First, I want to thank all the people who have contributed to me over my lifetime. From my pediatrician, Dr. Bugs Buganski, to my grade school basketball coach Bob Woods, my high school math teacher Mrs. Montgomery, my human resources director at Price Waterhouse, Mark Sherman, and my former boss, Joe Matson, to name just a few. I want you all to know that you have contributed to me, and in turn I contribute to others, and together we make the world a better place.

Several people thought I was crazy when I told them how quickly I wanted to create this book. I could not have done what I set out to do without a great team. While my name is credited as the author, it was an incredibly gracious, passionate and committed team that made this book a reality. I acknowledge the writing and research team of Sheila Mary Koch, Sandi Davis and our editor, Julie Sturgeon, and the graphic design team of Alan Kantor, Jeff Keifling and Jenny Glonek. I acknowledge the invaluable creative contributors, my mom, Carol Hall, my wife, Jennifer and my friend, Susan Rook. My team knows that this book is only the beginning of our journey together, and I truly appreciate and am amazed by their dedication. I also want to thank Kathlyn Hughes, Linda Ford and my mother-in-law, Sally Reece. Their contributions to the book made it one hundred times better than I could have ever imagined.

Finally, I thank my naiveté. Without it, I would miss many of the thrilling adventures life has to offer and I would not be able to produce the impossible.

Disclaimer

The recommendations presented in this book represent the opinions of the Author. The Reader follows these recommendations at his or her own risk. Neither the Author nor the Publisher makes any warranty of any kind, expressed or implied, about the usefulness, practicality, or safety of any of these recommendations. Neither the Author nor the Publisher assumes any liability whatsoever for the Reader's actions, whether or not those actions may be said to have been influenced by this book. If you are not willing to comply with these limitations, please do NOT read this book. You may return this book to the Publisher for a full refund.

Table of Contents

Birth of the Future Scrapbook

CHAPTER 1

"Keep true to
the dreams of
your youth."

Johann Fridrich Vom Schiller

Remember the dreams you had when you were younger? Maybe you saw yourself becoming President of the United States, a doctor, sports hero, movie star, or astronaut. Perhaps you wanted to end crime, stamp out world hunger, or save the animals in Africa.

> *destroy or extinguish by stomping with the boot*

When I was young, I wanted to be a restauranteur just like my grandfather. As I grew older, however, I focused on the high-risk business of restaurants rather than the thrill of creating exotic

> *excitement*

meals for my patrons and I gave up on my dream. A shift in focus often stops us from trying. We lower our expectations, often

> *degrade, Let down*

unconsciously. Yet our dreams remain with us, buried deep in our subconscious. This book has been created to help you explore and get back in touch with your dreams.

> *apparently*

The idea for the Future Scrapbook was born when a few seemingly unrelated events came together and presto! Much like a scientific discovery, I suddenly had something people wanted for themselves.

One December day in 1997, I was at my kitchen table working

> *to write hastily or carelessly*

through a personal goal-setting exercise. I scribbled away my dreams and goals, and although I enjoyed the process, the finished product - a list of dreams and goals on a piece of paper with written descriptions - didn't really inspire me. I was supposed to tape the list on my headboard and bathroom mirror, stick it in my day planner, and read the list every day. Frankly, my wife didn't think much of the new artwork in our house. Reading the list every day didn't inspire me, and eventually my dreams morphed into a creative but boring to-do list.

Dreamality - dreams locked away in your mind, converted to a physical format, and recognized as realistic by today's world.

A few weeks later I went home for Christmas and pulled out press clippings from my years as a star basketball player in my hometown. My favorite clipping is a detailed account of me driving the length of the court and making a shot that put our team into overtime for the league championship. Whenever I read that clipping, my adrenaline starts pumping as if I were again making that basket. Reading the story this time lit me up so much I called many of my old teammates to play basketball that afternoon!

About the same time I noticed several stories in the news about the popularity of scrapbooks. People host parties to assemble these crafts, relying on their old photographs and clippings. Like the thud of a ball bouncing off the backboard, it hit me: I could create a scrapbook about my future! I could have news clippings, pictures and articles of my future accomplishments that were as inspiring as the basketball clippings that propelled me into action! Instead of merely listing goals to describe what I wanted my future to look like, I could create a "dreamality" - concrete, realistic evidence that I had achieved those dreams. My Future Scrapbook would be as powerful and dynamic toward my future as clippings are of my past.

I was excited about this tool's possibility to express the dreams locked inside my head. I shared the idea with friends and others who I thought could help me complete my Future Scrapbook. What I didn't see at the time was how important it was for other people to get excited about my creation - and to offer to contribute to its completion. I was shocked at the reaction: They wanted a Future Scrapbook for themselves. I knew then that I needed share my concept with those wanting to take goal setting to another level or with those struggling to discover what they want out of life.

A dreamality from my original Future Scrapbook. The cover was originally 'GQ', but was changed for use in this book.

Within months, stories I had written in the scrapbook started to become a reality. For example, I created a template of an automobile license registration that listed my residence as San Francisco, California in 2001. In April 1998 my wife, Jennifer called from her business meeting in Chicago to announce she had a shot at a promotion ... in San Francisco. Having California in my Future Scrapbook provided me the clarity and commitment to say, "Yes, let's go!" without skipping a beat. Her company was shocked to get such a resounding 'yes' so quickly. Although it sounds almost magical, five months later and 18 months ahead of schedule, my dream of moving to California became a reality!

Jennifer and I often use the Future Scrapbook process to design what our family and relationship will look like. That is why my Future Scrapbook also includes a dreamality dated September, 2045, along with a picture of my wife and me. The caption explains how our four children threw a huge party to celebrate our 50th wedding anniversary. We both agreed that going on a date every week would be an important contribution toward that all-important anniversary party. Whether we grab an ice cream cone, rent a movie or go out to dinner, we make sure nothing stands in the way of our date. Many people go on dates with their spouses because they "should spend more time together." Jennifer and I go on dates because we have a dream.

Imagine the synchronistic events such a scrapbook could set into motion for you. Within the pages of my own Future Scrapbook, I placed my face on the cover of 'GQ' magazine. The cover reads "Nick Hall: Creating a Magical World with His Words." Just six months later, I was feeling especially tired on a flight from Cincinnati to San Francisco, not up to my usual tendency of chatting with the person sitting next to me. Finally,

Entrepreneur Appears on The Oprah Winfrey Show and The Today Show

Entrepreneur Nicholas Hall has appeared on The Oprah Winfrey Show and The Today Show recently sharing his Future Scrapbook. He, along with many of his friends in the writing and graphics trade, constructed a scrapbook based upon his goals and aspirations.

"I got the idea looking through one of my old scrapbooks. I realized that when people asked me about myself, I would answer by telling about my past instead of my future," Mr. Hall said. When he started to share his idea, he found support from many different areas. "The idea intrigued me," said Jill Schlarman, who has written for Mr. Hall since 1997. "It was great to work with his ideas and turn them into the concrete reality that he had imagined."

His explanation of this creative venture was summarized when he said, "Many of us have goals and aspirations, but they are a one-line sentence on a piece of paper or a thought that hits us every year on New Years. I wanted my goals to live and breathe and for people to relate to me as the future that I am living into, not my past. When they realize what I am up to, our conversation takes on a whole new meaning."

Mr. Hall has received inquiries from many people to have scrapbooks made for them. He is currently working with his writers and graphics friends to set up a company to service the many requests he has received.

"When people come to my office and see an article framed on the wall that has my future spelled out, it puts everyone in a powerful state of mind," Mr. Hall said.

Another dreamality from my original Future Scrapbook.

I eeked out a simple "Hello. How are you?" She turned out to be the person at GQ responsible for its covers.

For many, this may seem purely coincidental. However, I realized that by creating my Future Scrapbook, I became a magnet for the resources necessary to complete my dreams. I sent my seat companion a copy of the 'GQ' cover and now the powers-that-be there know who will grace their cover in March 2015. In fact, I contacted my seat companion last summer to report the progress of my Future Scrapbook. She instantly remembered me and helped to put me in contact with the editors at GQ!

Knowing that I am actively creating a compelling future brings a new level of excitement to my life. I am thrilled to share this excitement with you. Have fun creating your own Future Scrapbook!

A
Clear
Vision

CHAPTER
2

A plane flying to its destination is off course at least 90 percent of the time, yet thousands of planes reach their destination every day. Why? Because the course is charted and the goal is clear.

M any of us are like cars: We have lots of power and motion, but we're driving around in circles because we don't have a clear destination. We are so busy expending mental, physical and emotional energy, we forget to pinpoint a destination. A friend of mine who is a professional pilot revealed that a plane flying to its destination is off course at least 90 percent of the time, yet thousands of planes reach their destination every day. Why? Because the course is charted and the goal is clear. Or, for you golfers, I find myself off course at least 90 percent of the time. However, I never lose track of my destination - that cup on the green with the waving flag.

It is also easy to lose sight of our destination when we travel without roadmaps. We stray onto life's tangents and then wonder why we're stuck on an exit - longingly looking at the interstate we once craved. To compensate, we say, "Oh well, it was a dumb dream" or even worse, "I didn't really want that anyway." We scale down our dreams to fit into the box our life has become. But as quickly as you created the box that excludes your dreams, you can create a new box to include them! Your Future Scrapbook serves as your destination, so the ability to chart your course becomes clear.

Sandi, a good friend of mine, had a job for fourteen years that no longer excited her. It was drudgery. Creating a vision of the qualities she wanted for her future career, Sandi uncovered her deep desires for connection and for making a difference. Armed with this knowledge, she discovered personal coaching as a career. She fell in love with her first class and took a leap of faith with clarity of destination. This clarity, a career as a personal coach, provided Sandi the direction to support herself as a coach within six months.

"I always have to
dream up there against
the stars. If I don't
dream I will make it,
I won't even get close."

Henry J. Kaiser

I knew for many years I wanted to live in different places around the world. But while residing in Cincinnati, I created a limiting box I didn't recognize until I created my Future Scrapbook. You see, my career at that time made it difficult to move, but my Future Scrapbook detailed a life as an entrepreneur that would provide me the freedom and flexibility to live wherever I chose. So when the opportunity arose to move to San Francisco, I immediately shouted, "Yes!" even though it meant building a new network of friends and associates. My commitment to freedom and flexibility made the difference.

Challenge Imaginary Leashes

Achieving all we desire often means first releasing limited visions of ourselves. These may be beliefs we formed due to personal circumstances or what others have told us about ourselves. In either case, such beliefs are self-imposed and needlessly confining.

My neighbor's dog represents a great example of imaginary limits. The other day I saw the dog outside on its leash. The leash was tied to a stake lying in the driveway - it wasn't grounded to anything. Yet, the dog never ventured beyond the leash's reach. Amazed, I asked my neighbor why. He replied that at the previous house, the stake was driven into the ground. The dog still operates under the old rule, without challenging or testing its validity.

Be honest. Do you sometimes operate as if you are on an imaginary leash? Trying to determine what you're capable of accomplishing tomorrow based on yesterday's accomplishments or failures diminishes your potential. To become open to an unlimited future, it is important to look at the imaginary leashes we consciously and unconsciously place on ourselves.

Senior Business

April, 2007

Green Thumb Grannies Blooming

Eight years ago Anita Debonneville, age 81, founded Green Thumb Grannies, a booming garden and plant maintenance company, headquartered in Louisville. In that time, the company has gone from a local, one-woman operation to a successful enterprise with operations in several cities throughout the Midwest, including Lexington, Cincinnati, Indianapolis and St. Louis. Several more cities are slated to have offices very soon.

It is not everyday that a 73 year old starts a new business. "I probably would not have started this business if it wasn't for a dream that was burning inside of me," said Ms. Debonneville. "There was a house that I wanted so badly I could taste it, but I couldn't afford it. I thought the only way I was going to be able to get it was if I won the lottery. Then a friend of my granddaughter suggested turning my passion for gardening into a business."

Green Thumb Grannies has been a hit since the very beginning. What makes it special is that nearly all of the employees are senior citizens who work in people's gardens and in office buildings. "So many people my age die from loneliness, depression and lack of purpose. It is a great chance for our employees to get out and interact with other people while doing work they love," said Ms. Debonneville. "Personally, I feel such a connection with God when I am caring for gardens and plants that my energy level keeps going up."

And Ms. Debonneville's dream house? Last fall she moved into the beautiful new home that she dreamed about for so many years. When asked when she plans on retiring from the gardening business, Ms. Debonneville replied, "Never, I am going to live to one hundred and my family will be able to find me in my garden."

Currently Anita takes care of her friends' and family's gardens and lives in Louisville, Kentucky.

Break Through to a Compelling Future

Stand up and reach as high as you can - go ahead, give it a try. Reach as high as possible ... now reach a little higher. See, you can always reach a bit more. If you still don't believe me, call in a friend. Ask her to repeat the exercise while you measure the results. The amount higher may be small, but it exists.

This is great news when applied to our dreams, so allow yourself to dream beyond the limits of what you think you can and can't do. Stretch your dreams and something amazing happens - a quantum leap. Things become available that weren't possible before. We identify these invisible forces by many names: synchronicity, subconscious mind, mental imagery, intuition, luck. These could be aspects within yourself or a resource you previously overlooked.

For me, writing this book is a quantum leap. The odds were stacked against me. I was an accounting major in college - a numbers guy, not a writer! I have been busily engaged in starting a new company as well as serving as president for a local non-profit organization. I knew little about writing a book, how to go about layout, publication and marketing. What I did have was a clear vision of what was possible from writing this book - people living lives they love. When I started to share the vision of my book with others, an abundance of resources popped up in my life. Within one month, I had twelve people on my Future Scrapbook team who had all the skills and talents necessary to produce and distribute my book!

Think Outside the Box

The Future Scrapbook challenges us to look beyond ourselves and how we perceive the world. Experts generally agree that we

---

Playing it safe and cautious can kill the creativity and risk-taking necessary for success. Trying harder isn't necessarily the solution to achieving more. Sometimes it is a big part of the problem - it may even kill your chances for success.

---

reach only the tip of the iceberg of our true potential. Perhaps our common sense and logic keeps us from realizing our full potential. The conventional growth concept tells us that we must move systematically from our present level of achievement to the next, a gradual progress one step at a time. I did that for years. There's a lot to be said for slow and steady growth. But playing it safe and cautious can kill the creativity and risk-taking necessary for success. Trying harder isn't necessarily the solution to achieving more. Sometimes it is a big part of the problem; it may even kill your chances for success.

Consider, for instance, a bug attempting to sail through a windowpane. It bangs its head into the pane; it crawls along the surface, buzzing madly. Its strategy is to try harder to hurl through the glass. It has staked its life on reaching its goal through raw effort and determination. Now, we all know for the bug that it is impossible to try hard enough. How did it get so locked in on that particular route? What logic is there in continuing, until death, to seek a quantum leap with "more of the same"? Yet with only a fraction of the effort that bug is now wasting, it could be free of its self-imposed trap. The bug merely needs to find another entry, something dramatically different, like an open doorway. You may need to let go of preconceived notions on how to reach a goal.

This is not an argument against self-discipline or persistence. These are valuable assets. Sometimes staying power is the trait that delivers the results. However, combining persistence with creativity can give you the design of your life. I started my entrepreneurial journey four years ago. I knew I wanted to be an entrepreneur, but I had no idea what direction I would take. As a result I floundered for a couple of years, bouncing from idea to idea, not committed to any one in particular.

America's Youngest Investors

FORTUNATE

November 18, 2008

$4.00

Prestigious Ernst & Young Entrepreneur of the Year

Nicholas Hall has a simple formula for success...

Another Future Scrapbook original. I also wrote an article that goes into more detail about my simple formula for success.

When I created my Future Scrapbook, I knew accepting the prestigious Ernst & Young Entrepreneur of the Year award would illustrate one of my dreams. In the accompanying article I described my unique ability to bring revolutionary ideas to different industries. To date, my entrepreneurial journey has involved financial planning, food and beverage, consulting and high technology. Still, if you'd predicted in 1997 that I would create a company from scratch, I'd have thought you crazy. Creativity combined with persistence has given me the design of my life. Now if you accuse me of starting a revolution in an industry that I initially know little about - I'd say you know me like the back of your hand!

The Perspective of a Lifetime

My grandfather, Nicholas Graham, was born in Crete in 1899. He immigrated to the United States in 1915 and lived until the ripe old age of 91. The world created and accomplished things during his lifetime that he never could have even imagined as a young boy. Communication went from telegram to telephone, radio, television, fax, and e-mail. When my grandfather was born, horse-drawn carriages, boats and steam-powered trains transported people and goods. Now, automobiles, planes, bullet trains, and space travel are commonplace. All the modern comforts we take for granted in our homes - indoor plumbing, computers, refrigerators, washing machines and dryers - came on line during the past century. Every invention started with someone who said, "Hey, I think I can reach a little higher." So there is no reason to limit the possibilities for the future. Having the design of your life starts with reaching a little higher.

Birdies & Bogies

Business Tycoon Qualifies for Senior PGA Tour
July, 2020

By Jill Schlarman

Nicholas Hall is living out a dream he created many years ago. Competing against hundreds of talented golfers, Hall performed at his best on June 5th at the Pine Ridge Country Club in Raleigh, North Carolina.

During the last round of the final qualifying tournament for the Senior PGA Tour, Hall earned his card for the 2021 season. He is now preparing to face some of the most talented golfers in the world. Hall's rich background in golf has prepared him for the competition.

Golf has been a favorite pastime for Hall most of his life. "I learned to play golf when I was only seven years old", Hall said. His grandfather and namesake, Nicholas Graham, was an avid golfer and proved to be a role model for Hall.

"I was a golf junkie growing up, but for some reason I put the clubs down in high school," Hall admitted. "It was probably because it wasn't a "cool" sport like basketball", he said.

As Hall's success in the business world increased, his success in the golf world increased. He realized in his early adult years how much he loved the sport.

Regardless of his scores, he always thought of the golf course as a great place to be. At age twenty-seven Hall set the goal of playing on the Senior PGA Tour.

"I didn't know if the tour would even be around, but it was worth a shot," Hall said. What was it that pushed Hall's dream into reality? "What I was finally able to learn that put me over the top and gave me the chance to play on the tour was my mental stamina. I never truly appreciated how much of the game is mental," Hall said.

This breakthrough occurred in 2005 when Jack Nicklaus taught Hall how to play in the "present." "He taught me not to worry about my last shot or think about my next, but to be totally present to my current shot," Hall said.

Nicklaus, a mentor to Hall, has also become a friend who supported Hall through the qualifying tournament. "It was an honor and a privilege learning from the greatest golfer that has ever lived," Hall said.

Knowing that his goal was to qualify for the Tour, does he think he has a realistic chance of winning an event? Hall replied "Without a doubt."

I have a copy of this dreamality framed in my office with several PGA players' autographs on the article.

Create Dreamalities

A Future Scrapbook is a compilation of dreamalities. Dreamalities are dreams locked away in your mind converted to a physical format and recognized as realistic by today's world. For example, the article in my Future Scrapbook about me qualifying for the Senior PGA tour is a dream. This dream has been converted to a physical format - the article itself. And it is a realistic dream in today's world. People qualify to play on the Senior PGA tout every year. That's a dreamality.

Henry Ford said, "If you say you can, you can; if you say you can't, you're right." Science has shown that what we tell our brain affects our whole self. Positively stating what we want for our future activates the power of language. Creating a Future Scrapbook is a way of saying, "I can" to your dreams.

Language becomes even more powerful when it is written and shared. Take, for example, the promises I make to myself orally or silently in my head. I can't tell you how many times I made New Year's resolutions such as losing weight, spending more time with my wife, saving more money or taking an art class. If I followed through on my promises to myself, there would be no need to make the same resolutions year after year. But it is very easy to break promises we make to ourselves.

Instead, imagine taking your dreams as seriously as making your house payments. Contracts for business, marriage, loans, and insurance are basically promises written and signed with a witness. The contract binds you to following through on your promise because (A) it is in writing and (B) it offers concrete images as reminders. When my wife and I secured a loan for our house, we were very clear of the monthly payment and the

"The moment of
enlightenment is when
a person's dreams of
possibilities become
images of probabilities."

Vic Braden

consequences of not paying it. Still, our mortgage company sends us a visual reminder every month, just in case.

Shared written language and visual images get accomplished. The Future Scrapbook is a written and visual shared image for your future, a way of accomplishing what is really important to you.

Bring Your Dreams to Life

How many of us have read books on goal setting but still flounder? How many times have we written our goals only to shove the list into a desk drawer, never to be seen again? What about taping our goals onto headboards or bathroom mirrors, only to have them become permanent pieces of art? The Future Scrapbook gives you the ability to clearly articulate your dreams to yourself and others. It allows you to bring your dreams to life and give them a dimension that is missing when they are merely a list on a piece of paper.

Your dreamalities serve as real and believable evidence for your future. I keep a copy of my Future Scrapbook on my coffee table, next to my family photo album - one a display of my past, the other of my future. It provides an opportunity to share with people who I am and where I'm headed. And by sharing my aspirations with people, it enables others to contribute to my future. People who know about my dreams and goals will often, without even knowing it, hold me accountable to making my dreams a reality. It has been as simple as my wife's Aunt Norma asking how my singing lessons are progressing.

Your Future Scrapbook provides clarity of destination, giving you the tools to turn your dreams into dreamalities, for the design of your life!

Dream
Stoppers

CHAPTER 3

"A dream
is your creative vision
for your life in the future.
You must break out of
your current comfort zone
and become comfortable
with the familiar and
the unknown."

Denis Waitley

So if we know it is possible to be off course most of the time and still get to the right airport, why aren't our lives filled with smooth landings? We lack clarity of destination and we stop flying. But, a pilot doesn't say, "I'm off course, so I'd better land now." He makes the flight correction and continues.

I don't know about you, but I don't always keep going. Something derails me and I stop without a way to reach my destination. So let's look at what stops the action.

Fear

Many people assume they are the only ones afraid, that successful people feel no doubt or hesitation as they take on their dreams. Fear and doubt are common for people embarking on something new. Consider the amount of doubt and hesitation you feel as simply a measure of how far you are outside your comfort zone.

How many of us use the fear of failure as a reason for not trying? Dr. E. H. Land of Kodak points out that repeated failure in science is what makes this field successful. "When you work in the lab, you fail, fail, fail. When you have failed enough times, you have 3,000-speed film. If you want color film, you have to fail ten times as many times. Failure here is the very essence of progress. The secret of science is that it has learned to fail without emotion and embarrassment," he notes. Imagine what would be possible if you saw failure merely as a method of learning.

Some of us first encounter fear when we move towards what we desire. Sometimes that is as far as we go! Different things

Making a Difference
The Journal of Extraordinary People

August 2005

ROOK TAKES QUEEN

Washington, DC - The Presidential Medal of Merit goes to Susan Rook, noted author and motivational speaker. In a ceremony on the West lawn of the Capitol, the President veered away from her written remarks to say, "I used the Future Scrapbook to create a future for me where a woman President would not be unusual. Thank you for bringing clarity to my personal vision. Thank you, also, for the difference you make in the world and specifically with children."

Three Future Scrapbook Award Winners told of their journey from a predictable future to a future they designed. Dalleon Johnson said, "I'm going to college today to study veterinary medicine. Every time I wanted to stop in school and just give up, I went and looked at my vet degree in my future scrapbook. I see the articles written about my work with animals. It's real to me and I get my homework done today because I know where I'm going." Johnson's grandmother Annie White said, "I've always dreamed of owning my own home but when I saw it in print in the Future Scrapbook, it became real enough for me to actually get it. This is a blessing."

Nick Hall, wife, Jennifer and son, Graham shared the stage with Rook. Nick joked with the President saying, "It's nice to see the White House up close. I've got the Future Scrapbook entry when I'm President and I'm clear my dreams do come true!" Everyone laughed and Susan's husband, a noted documentary maker quipped, "Well, I'm around you guys all the time so I better start cataloguing the film library now! It'll be the fastest "making of a President movie" ever produced!"

From the halls of political power, the crowd of politicians and celebrities moved to the street celebration...dubbed, "Rook, Queen for a Day." Tasha Rodriguez, a teacher at a high school that boarders 14th street told of a time when this neighborhood was a scary place to work and live, "I would get nervous going to school. Can you imagine, nervous about going to school?" Today the school and the neighborhood are part of a revitalization project. Joe Ball, a local community activist, attributes the change to a community wide future scrapbook project, "Look around you, we're going someplace; we know where we're going, and we're getting there."

Rook saved her personal remarks for the street celebration. As she introduced her family to folks on the street, she said, "This is my award; this is my reward." She spread her hands, "I remember when this place was a crack house and that alley right there wasn't safe to walk in. Just look at that garden, look at those kids playing. This is my home." Rook's brother, an expert in wilderness medicine, dryly commented, "How are you going to top this?" Amid laughter, a woman pushed through the crowd and embraced Rook, "I knew I wanted a better life for my kids, I could dream big for them and now we're ALL dreaming big!" Rook's response, "All I've ever wanted to do was leave this world a little bit better than when I came in and to know my life had meaning. Looking at all our lives, I have my meaning."

Susan is a moderator, speaker and former host of CNN's Talkback Live. She is also the Public Relations Director for the Future Scrapbook.

generate fear. Imagine swerving to avoid a car pulling out in front of you. Now imagine making a call to ask someone you do not know for a business loan. Physiologically, you may feel the same in these two very different situations. Your heart beats faster and your adrenaline pumps. In the first scenario, your safety depends on listening to the cue to swerve. However, in the second situation, obeying your fear keeps you from getting what you need for your business. In both scenarios the feelings of fear look much the same. Pause to see what's happening beneath the emotion.

Fear disguises itself in many different ways. Learning to distinguish when you are afraid gives you more choices in how to proceed.

EXERCISE:

What do you do when you are afraid? _____

_____

_____

_____

_____

Do you stop taking action? _____

Do you resort to old habits? _____

Sometimes fear hides behind "tricks" such as getting so busy with mundane tasks that these tasks crowd out time to pursue dream projects.

-- -- -- -- -- -- -- -- -- -- --

Children don't have all of the junk attached to the word "no" that we do as adults. Children simply keep asking until they get what they want. Indeed, asking does make us vulnerable and being willing to be vulnerable is the essence of growth.

-- -- -- -- -- -- -- -- -- -- --

For many people, hearing "no" is a big fear. Beneath this fear may lie the notion that "If I ask, what will they think about me?" As adults, we convince ourselves it is better to not ask then risk potential humiliation or disappointment. People willing to ask for what they want are people who get more of what they want out of life. Children don't have all of the junk attached to the word "no" that we do as adults. Children simply keep asking until they get what they want. Indeed, asking does make us vulnerable and being willing to be vulnerable is the essence of growth.

EXERCISE

Let's take a look at the things you are afraid to ask for. List some of the scariest moments you can imagine, along with why you find them scary. The idea is to distinguish if your fear is essential to your safety or if it keeps you from having the design of your life.

For example:

Afraid to: *ask a friend on a date.*
Because: *I am afraid she will say no.*

Afraid to: *go skydiving.*
Because: *I am afraid the parachute might not work.*

Afraid to: *ask my friends to lend me money to start a business.*
Because: *I am afraid if I lose their money, that will end our friendship.*

Afraid to: _____

Because: _____

_____

"I'll do my dreaming with my eyes wide open, and I'll do my looking back with my eyes closed."

Tony Arata

Afraid to: _____

Because: _____

_____

Afraid to: _____

Because: _____

_____

Afraid to: _____

Because: _____

_____

Stating what we want outside of what is considered "regular and normal" can especially trigger the fear of what others will think. While your fear may be a realistic prediction of others' reactions, consider the alternatives. Being "regular and normal" can give you a very steady life, but that can be boring. There is a good reason why the biggest, fastest, and tallest roller coasters have the longest lines. They are outrageous rides and sometimes being outrageous is the most fun. Is avoiding the roller coaster of an outrageous future worth not having the design of your life?

Limiting Beliefs

By now you should recognize some areas where fear stops you, and how that limits you in having the design of your life. Next, let's look at the more subtle limiting beliefs - attitudes so much a part of who we are, that we don't notice their impact on our lives. Some limiting beliefs are widely accepted and supported in our culture, making it even more difficult to see them for what they are and to challenge them. We accept them as our personal

Pen & Ink

"Rocking the Cradle" — Top Pick for Holiday Season

November 20, 2005

The Editors' Top Pick this holiday season celebrates its sixth week as a New York Times Best Seller. *Rocking the Cradle* by Sheila Mary Koch is a fascinating true account of women leading communities out of poverty largely through the use of creativity and spirituality. Not only is it impossible to put down, the book will inspire even the most cynical that positive change is truly possible.

Readers report that they've been inspired to explore their creativity and get involved in their communities. The author has spent the last five years traveling to major urban areas and rural villages in the United States and Latin America to experience first hand the artistic and spiritual practices that are transforming entire communities. She got to know the people facilitating these changes, or as she says, "rocking the cradle." In the book, readers get to "meet" these inspirational artists and community organizers. "*Rocking the Cradle* is truly a cooperative effort, " said Sheila Mary. "While traveling, I glimpsed a depth of cooperation and community that is rare in the highly-developed technological world I come from. While technology has made so many things possible, we can not afford to devalue expression that comes from our hands and the kind of close community formed when we interact face to face." Consistent with the author's beliefs, fifty percent of the profits from the book go to the communities that made the book possible. In addition, Sheila Mary has formed the International Women's Coalition for Art and World Change with many of the women she met while working on the book. The organization brings women from many different disciplines and walks of life together to address pressing issues on a local and world scale. The group has been recognized by labor organizations and universities in Mexico, Cuba, Brazil, Peru, Guatemala and Venezuela.

Sheila Mary is an artist and writer.

reality and think they are based on rational thinking and an objective assessment of oneself. But limiting beliefs are the product of habitual, not accurate thinking. By accepting these warped ideas as reality, we doubt our abilities and our power.

Take a look at the following statements:

I'm old.

I'm young.

I'm a woman.

I started late.

I don't have money.

I have children.

I have a disability and have to work harder than other people.

If I am diligent and persistent, someday I will get what I want.

I don't deserve to get what I want.

I have already tried and failed.

The other person is more talented.

Maybe you do have children or you are older than recent college graduates. How you look at these facts and what you make them mean determines whether you allow them to limit you. To break free from limiting beliefs, start by stating the limiting belief, then the facts and then your negative judgment about the facts.

- -

EXERCISE:

Write at least five of your limiting beliefs.

For each limiting belief distinguish the facts and your negative judgment about the facts.

"Nothing is as real as a dream. The world can change around you, but your dream will not. Responsibilities need not erase it. Duties need not obscure it. Because the dream is within you, no one can take it away."

Tom Clancy

Example:

Limiting Belief: *I have difficulty following through to the end.*
Fact: *I have started three businesses in the last 5 years.*
Negative Judgment: *I am lousy at implementation.*

Limiting Belief: _____
Fact: _____
Negative Judgment: _____

Limiting Belief: _____
Fact: _____
Negative Judgment: _____

Limiting Belief: _____
Fact: _____
Negative Judgment: _____

Limiting Belief: _____
Fact: _____
Negative Judgment: _____

Limiting Belief: _____
Fact: _____
Negative Judgment: _____

Critical Inner-Voice

Our limiting beliefs are perpetuated on a daily basis by the critical inner-voice that whispers hosts of negative things about us. Our critical inner-voice is as individual as we are. It criticizes us and makes us feel bad about what we are doing ... or thinking of doing. It speaks very authoritatively about these truths. But it lies.

"To dream anything that you want to dream, that is the beauty of the human mind. To do anything that you want to do, that is the strength of the human will. To trust yourself, to test your limits, that is the courage to succeed."

Bernard Edmonds

The critical inner-voice is not your best friend or motivational speaker. A cunning creature, it knows how to get to you. If you try to banish it, it becomes still stronger and more clever. In fact, the critical inner-voice won't go away - it is part of being human.

Once you realize your critical inner-voice runs you - always trying to keep things on the same comfortable path it knows - you sail free to make empowering choices. But be warned: One guaranteed way to waken the critical inner-voice is to start moving toward a dream!

Stuck in the How-Tos

Creating the Future Scrapbook asks you to risk not knowing how your dreams will happen. If you say, "I will write a book," yet have never written more than a paper in school, it is natural to wonder how that will happen. Most likely, our future requires resources and skills that we do not possess today. This is to be expected. Trying to figure out how to get from here to there can lead to overwhelming feelings of hopelessness.

Trying to figure out your future based on your current resources and skills limits who you can be, what you can do and what you can have. After you create your Future Scrapbook, I will share a technique that gives you the ability to create powerful actions helpful to fulfilling your dreamalities.

Stuck in the Have-Tos

Sometimes we get stuck by the notion that what we choose for our future is carved in stone. We fear that if we state something, it becomes an expectation, and if we don't do it, we have failed. Nothing could be further from the truth. Writers throw out many

*I added this to my Future Scrapbook in September, 1999. I have been
a huge fan of Annie as long as I can remember. I love the message
that is delivered through the character of Daddy Warbucks, that the
"something" always missing for him was a family.*

characters and plots when creating a novel; artists paint over much when creating a masterpiece. You author whatever you create in your Future Scrapbook, so you reserve the right to change, modify or add to it.

The point of designing your future is not to measure accuracy or success versus failure. Some things you create in your Future Scrapbook may not happen because you change your mind. If you consider these possible scenarios a failure, it is easy to abandon trying.

Full Steam Ahead

If you see something that has stopped you in the past, creating your Future Scrapbook gives you an opportunity to leave it in the past. Challenging and overcoming your stoppers is a powerful part of your journey.

Thousands of entrepreneurs start businesses every year. Very few succeed. I started this book six months ago and at least four distinct times I truly wanted to quit. Then I pulled out my Future Scrapbook dreamality and read about the difference it made for people and was back in action. It allows me to get in touch with why I started this book in the first place. I also have an incredible support system of people who will not allow me to quit. They know about my commitment and vision for the Future Scrapbook and they want me to fulfill my dreams - almost as much as I do. What would be possible for you in your life if quitting were not an option?

I encourage you to reach out and communicate with other people when you are stopped. This action powerfully moves you beyond feeling alone. As you work through this book, find

----

What would be possible for you in your life if you stopped living like your life was only practice?

----

support outside yourself, including friends, family members, colleagues, associates and coaches. They can add value and support to the process and they can make it all more fun. Several friends helped me to complete my original Future Scrapbook. They were so excited and committed, it would have been impossible for me to quit before completion.

I don't focus on whether I achieve my future exactly as I state it - but stating my future empowers me to actively work toward its fulfillment. If you play for an outrageous future that requires something within you that you do not yet recognize, your journey will be lined with gold. The value of the Future Scrapbook is not the destination or achievement, but the journey that a self-created future provides.

In competition, athletes often perform at levels far beyond their achievements in practice. When competing for the gold medal in the Olympics, only one person in each event will win, but all the athletes' lives are impacted forever by the dedication and persistence it took to compete at that level. If we actively participate in our dreams, we'll engage at that higher performance level. Ask yourself, what would be possible for you in your life if you stopped living like your life was only practice?

Discover
Your
Dreams

CHAPTER 4

"Nothing happens unless first a dream."

Carl Sanburg

I t's playtime! Take on a childlike state of mind, where anything and everything is possible. Temporarily suspend your disbelief, and dream that you can be, do and have anything you desire! Rekindle childhood fantasies and invent new dreams.

Brain activity produces chemical reactions, which produce electrical fields. These different electrical fields result in different behaviors. Beta brain waves are typical in our daily living. In the beta wave state, we are programmed to be judgmental, concerned with the criticisms of others, concerned about performing for others and looking for approval from others. When the alpha waves are in control, we see 'what is.' We are interested in performing for ourselves. We look for approval from within and want to do our personal best instead of out-performing someone else. You might call this being in "the zone." For the upcoming exercises, you want to be in the zone. One thing you can do to reach this state of mind is to play calm and relaxing Baroque music with 50 to 70 beats per minute. You can find this music in your local music store; ask for the "Mozart effect" music.

So what are dreams? They answer the question, "What really excites me?" Dreams display an essence of who you are and inspire you to reach even higher. Dreams are different than goals. Goals are measurable - the stepping stones to make dreams come true. Yet, it is possible to have goals that don't lead to your dreams. Have you ever worked hard to accomplish a goal only to feel dissatisfied? Perhaps the goal was something you thought you should do. Or maybe you did it to please someone else. It probably wasn't connected to one of your true dreams.

CREATIVE PEOPLE

Disney and Divas Launch New Dolls

May 10, 2002

Superstar Natalie Cole, talk show host Oprah Winfrey and "Essence" magazine editor Susan Taylor will be the special guests at the Divas and Dolls launch party hosted by Disney's Michael Eisner and the New Doll Design Group at the New York City Marriott Marquis on May 12. Chief Executive Kathlyn Hughes will present each of the special guest divas with their own New Doll created by Chief Designer Mimi Hughes. The new doll design group is in partnership with Disney.

"We are extremely delighted to give our special guest divas the dolls that they inspired with their extraordinary generosity, talent and contribution to children," says Chief Engineer, Vicki Hughes. "Children are precious and these dolls represent possibility, promise and love for all our children around the world. We are excited about the opportunity to create a New Doll line for the Disney Group."

New Dolls are made of colorful fabrics and in all sizes. Like Raggedy Ann dolls with a cultural flair, they celebrate the diversity of the world's children. These unique collectibles were inspired by the three divas attending the upcoming celebration and the generous contributions they've made to children and the community. The dolls are meant to inspire children to love their families and friends, and to discover what is great about the world.

Disney's New Dolls will be available at Toys R Us stores all over the United States starting in September 2002 and can be ordered through the website NewDolls.Com just in time for the holidays.

Currently, Kathlyn works as a Business Analyst and Systems Designer for Health Systems Design, a health care information systems organization and lives in Castro Valley, California.

This chapter helps you get in touch with your dreams. This is not the time to break your dreams into goals or figure out how to make them come true. It is time to imagine that you cannot fail because you have every resource at your disposal. Suspend your beliefs about your capabilities. See yourself in a new light! Release yourself from what others may think!

Exploring Your Dreams

Schedule at least ten minutes when you can relax and focus for each exercise. You'll start to see exciting things about yourself after only one exercise if you truly allow yourself to dream like a child. If you find yourself being judgmental or impatient, take a break for a few minutes.

I encourage you to do these exercises with a buddy or small group. If you choose to do the exercises by yourself, plan to share the dreams you discover, especially the ones you are surprised to uncover.

- -

51 DREAMS

1. Take three pieces of paper or use the space provided.

2. Close your eyes and for sixty seconds imagine that you have unlimited time, money, talent, power, knowledge, support and self-confidence. Where would you be? What would you be doing? What would you do when you got up in the morning? What would it look like outside? Who would you communicate with during the day? What sort of work would you be doing? Would you be doing any work? What sort of contributions do you see yourself making to yourself,

"Where there is no vision, the people perish."

Proverbs 29:18

your family, your community, your country, and your planet? When you look around at your physical surroundings, what do you see? What are the colors and smells? What are the tastes in your mouth? Start to explore your entire lifetime. How long is your lifetime? What dreams will you pursue that keep you hungry to wake up for another day? Imagine that whatever you do, you can't fail!

3. Open your eyes and write a list of fifty-one dreams that you have for your life. Feel free to use the list provided on the following page. If you get stuck, repeat step two.

4. Be as specific as possible.

You may notice that your critical inner-voice gets in the way. You may start figuring out how to accomplish a dream. Or you may want to write, "Earn $1 million" but put down $250,000 just to be safe. That is the critical inner-voice's influence. When you notice this happening, acknowledge its existence and then dismiss it. Remember, dream with freedom - no one likes to be downsized!

You may begin to notice that the end of your list includes dreams you never before knew you had. Congratulations - you're thinking outside the box.

Here's an example:
1. Get into better physical shape.
4. Make money playing music.
7. Adopt a child.
13. Reduce the amount of violence in society.
21. Travel to a far-away place.
29. Teach children to play the violin.
34. Open a new school in my community.

America's Greatest Speaker Wins Fiancée

September, 2003

First place winner of the Toastmaster's National Speech contest, Jeffrey Keifling, has known fear. Having overcome the fear of public speaking after joining the TALK Toastmasters of Milford, Ohio in early 1996, 31-year-old Keifling has continually stepped up to take larger personal risks.

Sunday evening at the Toastmasters bi-annual National Speech contest in New York city, his risk taking paid off. He won not only the National title but also the hand of the woman he loves. Emotionally arousing his nationally televised audience, Keifling ended his speech with a proposal for marriage to his girlfriend of almost three years. She sat next to him during the thirty minute presentation, in which he talked about their love and the many experiences they have shared, yet the future bride never expected the speech to end in a marriage proposal. She overcame her surprise long enough to nod her head and say "yes."

"It's a speech I've wanted to give for a long time," says Keifling, "however, I wasn't sure how the response would play out in front of a large audience. It turned out very well; we're very excited."

Video clips of the speech and contest are available on NBC's web site, www.nbc.com. Keifling thanked Toastmasters, an international non-profit organization, for the opportunities that he has had to overcome his fear of speaking.

The couple will exchange their vows on January 31 with the scenic red rocks of eastern Arizona as a backdrop to Keifling's twenty-four acres of property. Later this month, Keifling, with his new speech, will move on to the international competition.

Jeff is the President of Graphic Strategy in Cincinnati, Ohio.

42. Learn and perform a Tahitian dance.

51. Organize a World Peace conference with over 50,000 people from twenty-five different countries in attendance.

Your 51 Dreams

1. _____

2. _____

3. _____

4. _____

5. _____

6. _____

7. _____

8. _____

9. _____

Remember there are no limits!

10. _____

11. _____

12. _____

13. _____

14. _____

What do you secretly want to do but have told no one?

15. _____

16. _____

17. _____

18. _____

19. _____

20. _____

Are there things you want to do that haven't been done before?

21. _____

22. _____

23. _____

24. _____

"We are what and where we are because we have first imagined it."

Donald Curtis

25. _____

26. _____

More than halfway there...Great work!

27. _____

28. _____

29. _____

30. _____

31. _____

32. _____

33. _____

34. _____

What is your escape fantasy?

35. _____

36. _____

37. _____

38. _____

39. _____

40. _____

41. _____

Only 10 more ... you can do it!

42. _____

43. _____

44. _____

45. _____

46. _____

47. _____

48. _____

49. _____

50. _____

51. _____

Congratulations!

"If a little dreaming
is dangerous,
the cure for it is not
to dream less
but to dream more,
to dream all the time."

Marcel Proust

Dream Storming

In case you decided that the last exercise wasn't for you or if you decided to read to the end of the chapter (and return later), here is another chance! If you did the last exercise, I invite you to complete this one, too, but feel free to skip it if you desire.

- - - - - - - - - - - - - - - - - - - -

EXERCISE

This exercise focuses on different areas of your life. Take at least five minutes in each area to brainstorm your dreams. Write everything that comes to mind - don't stop writing.

Personal Growth (what you want to learn, skills you want to acquire, fears you want to overcome, physical health and well-being you want to achieve, emotional and spiritual development you want to find)

_____

_____

_____

_____

_____

Career / Economic (yearly income, work goals, new business, impact on industry, retirement, net worth, etc.)

_____

_____

_____

_____

_____

"Everything starts as somebody's day dream."

Larry Niven

Fun, toys and adventure (travel destinations, things to create, purchase or do)

_____

_____

_____

_____

_____

Relationships (marriage, partnership, family, friendships, community)

_____

_____

_____

_____

_____

Contribution (what you want to do to make the world a better place, to give back to society, donate, volunteer)

_____

_____

_____

_____

_____

Your Perfect Day

This is one of my favorite exercises. This exercise is very different from the previous two because you won't be compiling a list of dreams. Instead, you will be seeing yourself as you make your

Future Scrapbook Technology Becomes Most Widely Used Tool in Business and Education

March 27, 2002

What started out as a simple way to make goal-setting more fun has become the most prolific tool used in business and education today. Nick Hall, creator of the Future Scrapbook and Chairman of Designerlife, wanted an easier way to stay connected with his dreams and to share his dreams. By creating realistic, physical evidence for future dreams, called dreamalities, people find themselves emotionally connected to their dreamalities and have a simple way to share their dreamalities with others. "I was frustrated that when I would meet someone new and we would talk about ourselves, we would always share from the past. I thought it would be very powerful to share with people about our future as a new way of getting to know someone." said Mr. Hall.

Altering How Corporations Operate

It is not uncommon to find two people at lunch sharing their Future Scrapbook. In fact, many companies do not take a single action on a project until they have created their Future Scrapbook dreamality. "It is such an effective tool that enables everyone involved in a project to have ownership and know that their contribution will make a difference." said Bill McKay, CEO of Microsoft. Vision and mission statements have been replaced by Future Scrapbook dreamalities. "It seemed odd that for so many years vision and mission statements were more likely catchy than meaningful to the organization, but nobody would say anything about it." added Michelle Olia, CEO of IBM, "Now we have an awesome dreamality that has juice and energy so that people inside and outside of IBM can read and watch and really get emotionally connected to our future."

The Future Scrapbook technology has evolved as well. What started out as simple templates and magazine headers on a cd-rom has grown into sophisticated software programs and videos. "It is so exhilarating to create a video of the future of our company in 2040. When I closed my eyes I could see exactly what it looked like, but the Future Scrapbook gave me the opportunity to share it with everyone in the company." said Anwar Milton of Evolutionary Designs, a startup in Boston.

Impacting Education

Several of Mr. Hall's original team members had a grand vision for the difference this could make in education.

Mr. Hall's mother, Carol Hall, is still traveling around the world bringing the Future Scrapbook technology to educational institutions. "We have brought the technology to educational institutions around the world, from most renowned universities to one room school rooms. This technology crosses cultures, language and educational levels. Every person has passion inside of him. The Future Scrapbook brings this passion out and lets him dream for the future." said Mrs. Hall.

Children in schools all across America start their school year by creating their own Future Scrapbook. "It is so neat to see how my Future Scrapbook has evolved over the years. I can actually see how every year my dreams get bigger and my future looks more exciting. Grade cards are fine, but Future Scrapbooks are cool." said Malik Thomas, a six grader in Chicago, Illinois. The Future Scrapbook brings hope to children who never had hope. Susan Rook, who sits on the advisory board of Designerlife, was the catalyst that introduced the Future Scrapbook technology to schools and local communities. In 2005 she was awarded the Congressional Award in Education for the program that dramatically altered the 14th Street community in Washington D.C. "If you asked me if I thought that what we did for that community would have the impact it has had on communities around the world, I would have said "absolutely." I would have said absolutely because we had created this future in our scrapbook." noted Mrs. Rook.

Creating Communities Based on Common Futures

For Mr. Hall, the most exciting result of the Future Scrapbook has been the creation of communities based upon common futures. It has created a breakthrough in mentoring programs throughout the world. "When young people have the opportunity to articulate what they see in their future, it helps us find the right mentor for them." notes Amy Rydell, executive director of Youth Works Foundation in Washington D.C.

What is next for Designerlife? Look no further than their own Future Scrapbook. Next year they brought together leaders from around the world to create the future of our planet. Maybe I could get them to include me as the reporter.

I created this dreamality in June, 1999.

way through your perfect day. You will be amazed at what you see and how quickly your mind takes you to your perfect day. You can repeat this exercise many times because you may find, like me, that you have several "perfect days".

EXERCISE

First, close your eyes. Imagine your perfect day. This is a day anytime in your future and anything is possible. Visualize your surroundings as you wake up, with whom you interact, and what activities you do.

Next, open your eyes and write what you imagined. Continue visualizing through your day, listing everything you do, feel, have and are. Write for at least ten minutes.

Now, highlight items that represent your dreams. For example, picking up your children from school may point to a dream of having a family. Going for a run first thing in the morning on the beach could represent your commitment to health and well-being as well as where you want to live.

_____

_____

_____

_____

_____

_____

_____

_____

_____

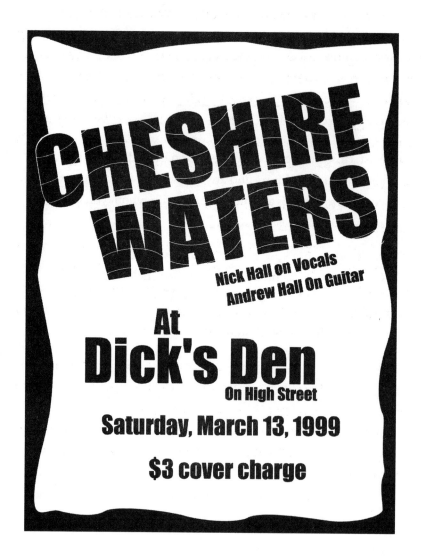

This was in my original Future Scrapbook and is an example of a dreamality that did not take placed as planned, but I am still in action taking voice lessons and practicing regularly.

One of my perfect days includes waking up in a big, soft, white bed with fluffy pillows and a warm comforter. I enjoy a nice run along the beach with my wife, Jennifer, and the family dog. I sip a fresh cappuccino in our spacious, stainless steel kitchen. I take a shower in a colorful, open tile shower with a giant window looking out towards the ocean. I join our children for breakfast before they go to school. I then drive to my office, just a few minutes away, and hold meetings or conversations with the CEOs of the many companies that I have founded. I return home for a relaxing lunch with my wife, then sprint to the golf course to play nine holes. I finish in time to pick up the kids from school. I have a great time cooking dinner for the entire family. I spend time playing with the kids before they go off to do their homework. I spend the next hour in my home office making calls to the CEOs in different time zones. I kiss the children good night and retire to the bedroom where Jennifer and I enjoy a glass of wine in front of a roaring fireplace.

Now that you have completed your dream brainstorming, it is time to revisit your lists from the three previous exercises and pick the dreams that really get your juices flowing. Take a highlighter over the 30 dreams that really light you up! Keep your highlighted dreams handy. You will return to them at the end of the next chapter.

Get in Touch with Your Passion Pushers

Passion Pushers represent what gets your adrenaline pumping and your juices flowing. Passion pushers are not chosen; they are intrinsic to you.

C hances are, the things in your life that truly make you happy express what I call your "passion pushers". Exploring your passion pushers is as important as discovering your dreams. If you have pursued dreams that aren't aligned with your passion pushers, you may have experienced emptiness when the dreams were fulfilled. Certain experiences are fundamentally important to us, so a life built upon our passion pushers is engaging and fulfilling.

Passion pushers represent what gets your adrenaline pumping and your juices flowing. Passion pushers are not chosen; they are intrinsic to you. People commonly confuse passion pushers with the things or people that provide them. For example, if you feel alive and fulfilled when spending time with your grandchildren, you may say, "My grandchildren are my passion pushers." Although spending time with your grandchildren may bring out a passion in you, look for the essence of what being with your grandchildren brings you. The passion pusher may be connection with family, the love you feel or the vitality you experience. The key is that a passion pusher is a principle rather than a thing. For instance, power is a passion pusher, rather than money, love rather than family, and fun rather than vacations.

Passion pushers are not static. Their intensity shifts at different times during our lives. However, because passion pushers are fundamental to who we are, they remain fairly consistent throughout our lives. For example, connection with family and exploration may be two of your passion pushers. In your early twenties, you may want to explore the world and work on a ship. In your thirties you may get married and go to the zoo

Micromite Corporation

January 8, 2007

Mr. Nicholas Hall
1000 Park Avenue
New York, NY 10001

Dear Mr. Hall:

I had the opportunity to read the recent article on your accomplishments in "The Wall Street Journal." I find it fascinating that you are able to be so successful in business and spend so much of your energy in other areas that many of us only dream about. I, like many other entrepreneurs, find myself spending all of my time trying to build my business. Now, I am beginning to realize that it is costing me all the things that are important to me.

It must have been difficult for you to keep from working all of the time because there is such a stigma about entrepreneurs and "wearing your business on your shirtsleeve." It would be a wonderful contribution to other entrepreneurs if you could share how you have been able to be and do everything that many of us cannot achieve because of different obstacles in our own lives.

I realize that you are extremely busy and have a tremendous amount of responsibility, but I would love to have the opportunity to meet you. I would enjoy talking to you and would like to find out what has enabled you to be so successful and make such a difference for people everywhere. Please contact me if you find time in your schedule.

Sincerely,

Bill Turner

Bill Turner

Another original Future Scrapbook dreamality. I often write letters to people I want to get to know. This letter represents entepreneurs asking me for assistance, something I look forward to receiving.

with your children, in your fifties buy a second home and in your sixties you may retire, only to explore the world again.

Examples of Passion Pushers

Review the list of common passion pushers. Add any of your passion pushers missing from the list. Now, review the list again and pick your personal top ten passion pushers, the ones most important to you.

COMMON PASSION PUSHERS

Rank PASSION PUSHER	Rank PASSION PUSHER	Rank PASSION PUSHER
___ Accuracy	___ Focus	___ Peace
___ Achievement	___ Free Spirit	___ Performance
___ Adventure	___ Freedom	___ Personal Growth
___ Aesthetics	___ Fun	___ Personal Power
___ Altruism	___ Growth	___ Powerful
___ Authenticity	___ Harmony	___ Privacy
___ Autonomy	___ Health	___ Productivity
___ Beauty	___ Honesty	___ Recognition
___ Bonding	___ Humor	___ Resolute
___ Certainty	___ Independence	___ Resolve
___ Clarity	___ Integrity	___ Risk Taking
___ Collaboration	___ Intimacy	___ Romance
___ Commitment	___ Joy	___ Security
___ Community	___ Lack of Pretense	___ Self-Expression
___ Completion	___ Leadership	___ Sensuality
___ Comradeship	___ Loyalty	___ Service
___ Connecting	___ Magic	___ Solitude
___ Contribution	___ Mastery	___ Spirituality
___ Creativity	___ Meaning	___ Success
___ Directness	___ Moderation	___ To Be Known
___ Elegance	___ Nature	___ Tradition
___ Emotional Health	___ Nurturing	___ Tranquility
___ Empowerment	___ Openness	___ Trust
___ Environment	___ Orderliness	___ Vitality
___ Excellence	___ Participation	___ Well-Being
___ Excitement	___ Partnership	___ Zest
___ / _____	___ / _____	___ / _____
___ / _____	___ / _____	___ / _____

"We've removed the ceiling above our dreams. There are no more impossible dreams."

Jesse Jackson

Next, find a photo of yourself doing something that made you feel particularly proud or content. If you do not have such a photo, close your eyes and imagine what you were doing.

What in that experience made you feel good about yourself?

_____

_____

_____

Where were you? _____

_____

_____

How old were you? _____

_____

_____

What was special about that experience? _____

_____

_____

What were you doing? How did you feel? _____

_____

_____

Who said what to you? _____

_____

_____

What was the expression on your face? _____

_____

_____

Passion Pushers

Risk Taking

Dreams

Entrepreneur
of the year

Passion Pushers

Self Expression

Passion Pushers

Connecting
with People

Dreams

Singing in
Public

Passion Pushers

Fun

I have a picture of when I was twenty-three and I visited my relatives on the island of Crete where my grandfather was born. It was an expression of two of my most powerful passion pushers: adventure and relatedness. My relatives were very proud of my family's accomplishments and appreciative that I made the effort to connect with them. I remember a permanent grin on my face the entire time I was there.

Are Your Dreams and Passion Pushers Aligned?

As a final step, examine your dreams and passion pushers to see if your dreams are an expression of your passion pushers. If they are not aligned, then chances are achieving your dreams will leave you unfulfilled. You also may notice that you have passion pushers without dreams to express them. In this case, feel free to create new dreams!

You have probably noticed from my Future Scrapbook dreamalities that I am a passionate entrepreneur. When I did this exercise, I found that my dream of receiving a letter from a promising entrepreneur requesting my help was an expression of three of my passion pushers - empowerment, independence and contribution.

Create a graph similar to the example on the preceding page to visualize the alignment of your dreams and passion pushers. You may notice, as the graph shows, that one dream can be expressed in several passion pushers.

Design Your Life

CHAPTER 6

"All human beings
are also dream beings.
Dreaming ties all
mankind together."

Jack Kerouac

W
e will now bring your dreams together to begin the process of living a life by design. You have the opportunity to create powerful Future Scrapbook dreamalities that bring your dreams to life. The process includes locating your dreams at specific dates and times in your future, and meeting the roving reporter who helps you add vivid details to your dreams.

Remember, you don't need to know all the "how tos" for having the design of your life, but you do need to know where you want to go. It is crucial to have a crystal clear picture of what you want to accomplish. If you rivet your attention on that landing spot, you'll magnetize yourself to the ways and means to get there.

The Process

As you begin the process of turning your dreams on a piece of paper into vivid, real and believable accomplishments, you may notice that it doesn't turn out to be a step-by-step process. In fact, the human brain doesn't function step by step, so feel free to jump around. Sometimes the process may feel messy and disorganized. Take heart, quantum leaps often occur in the messy and disorganized times of our lives! I have had great insights while cleaning the house!

- -
CREATING YOUR DREAMALITY

1. Before you start, I suggest having scraps of paper, different color markers or pens and space on your floor.

"Don't be afraid of the
space between your
dreams and reality.
If you can dream it,
you can make it so."

Belva Davis

2. Write each of the thirty dreams you highlighted from Chapter Four on a different piece of scrap paper and scatter the thirty pieces of paper on the floor. Even the act of writing down your dreams helps move them into reality. Research has shown that we are six times as likely to remember something if we write it down.

3. Your mission is to create a timeline for your dreams. Create six- to twelve-month increments over the next three years; then write five-year increments for the next twenty-five years; and then ten-year increments for as long as you would like. I actually have a 150-year goal, so don't quibble over reality versus fantasy. In fact, it may be empowering to imagine what future generations will say about you. We don't know how long we will live, but a compelling future can help keep us hungry for another day.

4. Place all your dreams where you think they should go on the timeline.

5. Look for gaps where there are no dreams and years where many dreams are grouped together. Remember also that your critical inner-voice is often disguised in the term "realistic." At the same time, many of us overestimate what we can accomplish in a year and underestimate what we can accomplish in a decade. The point is not when or if you accomplish your dreams, but rather the life you gain by reaching for them!

6. Look for inconsistencies. For instance, you may want to contribute $1 million to cancer research in 2008, but you didn't generate the income to make that contribution until 2012. In this case, you may want to move up the date you

UNIVERSE Tomorrow

Get all the news before it happens

Hall Foundation Donates $1,000,000 to Heart Research

April 5, 2005

By Jill Schlarman

In a formal ceremony, entrepreneur Nicholas J. Hall presented a million-dollar check written to The Lown Cardiovascular Clinic. Accepting the generous amount on the stage at Boston Dining Hall was a five-year-old heart patient, Zachary Johnson, and clinic chairperson, Dr. Bernard Lown.

The presentation was touching as Mr. Hall made a short speech and shook the hand of Dr. Lown and hugged Zachary, who is currently receiving treatment at The Lown Cardiovascular Clinic.

This is the second commitment of $1 million that the Nicholas J. Hall Family Foundation has made in the last month. On March 1, the Hall foundation contributed $1 million to Indiana University Hospital in Indianapolis. The two heart centers have a special place in Mr. Hall's heart, both figuratively and literally. Diagnosed with Wolff Parkinson White Syndrome as a child, Mr. Hall has a special connection with these institutions. As a result of the severity of his disease, Mr. Hall needed treatment from the premiere cardiac centers in the country. He spent time at The Lown Cardiovascular Clinic as well as Indiana University Hospital, which has led him to want to help the places that helped him so much as a child.

"What they did for me and what they have done for thousands of other people is a series of constant and never-ending miracles," Mr. Hall said.

Established in 2004, The Hall Foundation began with a contribution of $5 million from Mr. Hall. That contribution represents approximately 10% of Mr. Hall's estimated net worth. "Our family hopes that the foundation will continue to grow and prosper and to be able to bestow gifts that have a significant impact on the health and well-being of humans all over the world," Mr. Hall said after the ceremony.

"As both chairman of this clinic, and as a doctor, I am very appreciative of this charitable act. It means a great deal to me that Mr. Hall himself has been part of our center. He has been helped by the Lown Clinic and has taken it upon himself to help the clinic in return. I take pride, and feel I have a bit of responsibility for all he is doing in this world," Dr. Lown said.

This is my favorite dreamality and still gives me goosebumps and tears when I read it.

earn the income or move back the date of the contribution. The right move is the one that empowers you.

7. Once you have completed arranging your dreams on the timeline, step back and enjoy your accomplishment. You have taken a giant leap toward having the design of your life!

The Roving Reporter

Next, let's craft your future in more detail. Combining several dreams transforms this from an exciting list to an exciting life. I'll use one of my dreamalities from my original Future Scrapbook as an example. I had created three separate dreams and accomplishments for 2005: (1) A Hall family foundation was established, (2) A contribution of $1 million to heart research and (3) An accumulation of a personal net worth of $50 million.

In this exercise, imagine that an investigative reporter approaches you. The detail-oriented reporter wants to interview you and other people associated with your accomplishments to help readers feel as if they were there.

When the reporter asked where I was in 2005, I saw myself at a formal reception to make a presentation of my $1 million contribution to Dr. Bernard Lown, founder of the Lown Cardiovascular Clinic in Boston, Massachusetts. At my table were my parents, wife, two children and a five-year-old patient of the clinic. (Not coincidentally, doctors discovered my own heart condition when I was at that age.)

You may want to role-play with a friend to give this exercise an

"The best way to predict the future is to create it."

Source Unknown

authentic feel. Below are some of the basic questions the reporter asks you; tailor them to your specific situation. Write your answers on a notepad or, if you role play, record the interview.

First, the reporter needs to establish the basics: who, what, where, when, why and how. I will use my answers as an example.

Describe who you are and why you are here: *I am an entrepreneur. I grew up with a heart condition and received treatments at the institutions receiving my contribution.*

What are you doing and how are you able to do this? *I created a very successful business that gave me the ability to create a family foundation.*

Who are you with and why? *I am with my parents, wife and two children. There are also about one-hundred people in attendance, including Dr. Lown and several physicians from the clinic.*

What are you doing? *I am presenting a check for $1 million to the Lown Cardiovascular Clinic.*

What is the significance? *The Lown Cardiovascular Clinic was instrumental in the care and cure of my heart condition.*

How are you affecting other people in the world? *The family foundation was created to improve the health and well-being of humans all over the world.*

Where are you in terms of country, state, city? *The reception takes place in Boston, Massachusetts at the Boston Dining Hall.*

California
C i t i z e n

CITIZEN OF THE YEAR AWARD FOR VISIONARY

June 12, 2004

"CedNumber1 is a true renaissance man of the 21st Century", exclaimed Oakland's Mayor Jerry Brown, "in the mold of Leonardo Da Vinci". Those were just a few of the glowing comments heaped upon Cedric Long in Oakland's Citizen of the Year presentation. The ceremony took place in Oakland's famed Paramount Theater.

"The Visioneering Learning Method was a true Godsend for the Oakland Public Schools. I'm grateful the school district had the vision to implement it as a core element in our curriculum two and a half years ago", said George Musgrove, the school district's superintendent. "For Oakland's entire K-12 program to be in the top 5% of schools in the country this year is an amazing feat. And the parent and community involvement that The Visioneering Power Network Voice Mail Program has generated is nothing short of a miracle."

The Visioneering Learning Method combines several innovative techniques that are key components of an accelerated learning curriculum that has students thriving. It has proven so effective that California is going to have it implemented statewide in all public schools this coming school year.

"I'm so grateful for the Divine expression of Spirit to utilize me in this way. And I'm thankful that The Grace of God has empowered me to behold that Divinity in others too, especially our children;" commented Mr. Long in some words of acceptance, visibly moved by the ceremony. "CedNumber1 is in da house! And Love Magic is in the air!" he said, referring to his self-given moniker and multi-platinum Grammy award winning CD".

Co-author of The Einstein Factor (now a classic in the education field) Win Wenger commented in an interview after the ceremony, " for so many elements from The Einstein Factor to be integrated in a structured curriculum was a stroke of pure genius."

Currently Cedric operates his business, The Visioneering Power Network, a voice mail broadcast/ management company. He lives in Oakland, CA.

Why did you set this goal? *I wanted to contribute to people who made a significant contribution to my life.*

How did you accomplish this? *I contributed $5 million to my family foundation, which represents approximately ten percent of my estimated net worth. The $1 million contribution to heart research came from this fund.*

Here are some additional questions the reporter might ask you:

How does this feel to you?
Look around - what do you see? smell? hear? taste?
What are your emotions?
Are you smiling, crying or laughing?
From where did you arrive?
Were you invited?
Did you create this place or occasion?
What year is it?
What time of year and what day?
What else is happening in the world at this time?
How old are you?
Why is this important to you?

The questions appropriate for your dreams may trigger more questions. Certain dreams require a different focus. If you are writing about a charity benefit that you will host at your new dream home, describing your setting is important because the story is as much about your home as it is about the event. Include the senses in your description: sight, sounds, birds and wind through the trees, the smell of the trees and gardens, the taste of the food served, etc. For the charity benefit part of the dreamality, describing how it feels and why you did it is important because

"Success–To laugh often and much; to win the respect of intelligent people and the affection of children; to earn the appreciation of honest critics and endure the betrayal of false friends; to appreciate beauty; to find the best in others; to leave the world a bit better, whether by a healthy child, a garden patch or a redeemed social condition: to know even one life has breathed easier because you have lived. This is to have succeeded."

Ralph Waldo Emerson

both point to your passion pushers. In this example, see how you can also choose to express your career accomplishments, wealth, status, family, your friends ... the list is endless!

This reporter wants to be thorough and may also call others related to the dream. Who are the key people in your dream? Your spouse, friends, colleagues, recipients of what you did, industry experts, your parents, the mayor, a competitor, your children? What would these people say about you and your accomplishment?

In my example, Dr. Lown was very appreciative and proud of the fact I took it upon myself to give back. He also felt that because he helped me get a healthy heart, he has some ownership in the difference I am making in the world.

Review your notes. Do they include a date, setting, action, event, people, quotes, feelings, recognition, accomplishment, and details that excite the senses? If so, you have enough to create a dreamality for your Future Scrapbook. Continue to repeat the roving reporter process with other dreams.

Finally, I took all of my notes and began to craft the complete dreamality. Some of you may be thinking, "I can't write. My grammar, spelling, etc. is terrible." Keep taking action and write the dreamality anyway as a part of the creative process. Solicit input from people around you. We will talk more about the value of sharing in the next chapter.

You also may find that a picture or symbol would more accurately represent your future. In order to simplify the process, in the resource section of this book you will find information on how to purchase a Future Scrapbook CD-rom that includes templates and mastheads, many like those you see in this book.

CALIFORNIA DEPARTMENT OF HEALTH
DIVISION OF VITAL STATISTICS
CERTIFICATE OF LIVE BIRTH

Reg. Dist. No.   85   Registrar's No.   78956
Primary Reg. Dist. No. 0008   Birth No. 158-99-062848

CHILD-NAME First Middle Last	DATE OF BIRTH	HOUR
Graham Nicholas Hall	May 4, 2001	9:15 A.M.

SEX	THIS BIRTH-Single, Twin, Triplet	IF NOT SINGLE BIRTH-born first, second, third, etc.	COUNTY OF BIRTH
Male	Single		Contra Costa

CITY, VILLAGE OR LOCATION OF BIRTH	INSIDE CITY LIMITS	HOSPITAL-NAME
Walnut Creek	Yes	John Muir Medical Center

MOTHER-MAIDEN NAME First Middle Last	Age (At time of this birth)	State of Birth
Jennifer Rebecca Reece	28	New Jersey

RESIDENCE-STATE	COUNTY	CITY, VILLAGE, OR LOCATION	INSIDE CITY LIMITS	STREET AND NUMBER
California	Contra Costa	Walnut Creek	Yes	19000 John Drive Castro Valley

FATHER-NAME First Middle Last	Age (At time of this birth)	State of Birth
Nicholas John Hall	31	Ohio

Informant's Name or Signature	Relation to Child
Jennifer Hall	Mother

I certify that the above child was born alive at the place and time and on the date stated above.	DATE SIGNED	ATTENDENT-M.D., D.O., OTHER
SIGNATURE		M.D.

CERTIFIER-NAME	MAILING ADDRESS (CITY, STATE, ZIP)
William T. Bucknell	19000 John Drive Castro Valley

REGISTRAR-SIGNATURE	DATE RECEIVED BY LOCAL REGISTRAR

Our family planning became much clearer after we created this future.

The previous page shows the birth certificate my wife and I created for the birth of our first child two years into the future!

Whether an article, picture, symbol or combination of visual elements, the critical point is to transfer your list of dreams into dreamalities. When a dream becomes something you can believe, it becomes something you can achieve.

Take Action with Your Future Scrapbook

CHAPTER 7

Design-A-Life – A series of actions and stepping stones to turn your dreamalities into realities; this serves as your map, guiding you to your destination.

B y creating your Future Scrapbook, you have taken a powerful series of actions, setting yourself on an exciting new course and propelling unseen forces into motion. But hold on - the ride of your life has just begun! Most likely you tried new ways of doing things to create your Future Scrapbook. As you begin your journey into your life with your Future Scrapbook by your side, you will continue to find yourself taking uncommon approaches towards your dreams - actions outside your habits and routines.

Give yourself a big pat on the back! Being specific about your dreams can be challenging. It is estimated that only five percent of the population has clearly defined dreams. By creating vivid dreams, you choose to live a life by design.

A group of university business school alumni set out to determine how they were progressing toward their goals ten years after graduation. Amazingly, eighty-three percent of the graduates had set no goals at all. This eighty-three percent reported they were working hard and staying busy but had no specific future plans. Another fourteen percent had mental, but not written goals. However, this fourteen percent earned, on average, three times the income of those that had no goals. Only three percent of the entire graduate group had written goals, and that three percent earned a whopping ten times more than what those with no goals earned.

Later in this chapter, you will create a Design-A-Life, which is a series of actions and stepping stones to turn your dreamalities into realities. Your Design-A-Life serves as your map, guiding you to your destination. Here we encounter a paradox. You create a step-by-step structure for your life - a complex, unpredictable

Who's in the News

Mr. and Mrs. Nicholas and Jennifer Hall celebrated their 50th wedding anniversary with a reception given by their four children, Graham, Zachary, Taylor, and Cassandra` at the New York City Country Club. Many of their closest friends from around the world were in attendance. The picture above is from their wedding day, September 23, 1995.

This dreamality illustrates my dream of a wonderful marriage, a big family and being a world citizen.

process filled with quantum leap and seemingly unrelated occurrences. It is impossible to know all of the actions that you will take toward your dreams at the onset. While it may seem silly to use a map for something impossible to map, your Design-A-Life is critical because it gets you into action. Focused, directed action towards your dreams is the key to bringing them to life.

Remember that an airplane is off course ninety percent of the time and still reaches its destination. If you find yourself off course, you are exactly where you are supposed to be. Without being off course, you couldn't tell when you're on!

Turn back to the exercise in chapter five that aligns your dreams and passion pushers. In your Design-A-Life you will create measurable results whose manifestation is your dreams fulfilled. It is possible some of your dreams are already in the form of measurable results. Measurable means you can quantify the result. You have mile markers or signposts, such as dates and amounts, to help you know you have accomplished your dream. When I did my brainstorming exercises, I identified driving a Jaguar as a dream. To make that a measurable result, I identified the date that I would be behind the wheel. I turned my dream of living around the world into a measurable result by pinpointing what cities I would live in and during what years.

My wife and I dream of a passionate and nurturing marriage. The only problem is that this dream is not measurable, so it had always been difficult to know if we were both experiencing a dream marriage. We decided to create measurable results. One of our commitments is to go on at least one date each week that rates at least a six on a scale of ten on our "passion meter." Now we know whether we both are experiencing a dream marriage, and we are well on our way to celebrating our 50th wedding anniversary!

1040

Department of the Treasury - Internal Revenue Service
U.S. Individual Income Tax Return **2098**

IRS Use Only - Do not write or staple in this space

For the year Jan. 1 - Dec. 31, 2098 or other tax year

OMB No. 0000-0073

LABEL
(See instructions on page 10.)

Use the IRS Label. otherwise, please print or type.

Your first name and initial: Nicholas J.
Last name: Hall
Your social security number: 111 22 3333

If a joint return, spouse's first name and initial: Jennifer R.
Last name: Hall
Spouse's social security number: 333 11 2222

Home address (number and street). If you have a P.O. box, see page 10.
21 Redlands Airway
Apt. no.

City, town or post office, state and ZIP code. If you have a foreign address, see page 10.
Crater Falls, Mars CF-21

For help in finding line instructions, see pages 2 and 3 in the booklet.

Filing Status

Check only one box.

Exemptions

If more than six dependents, see page 10.

Income

Attach copy B of your Forms W-2, W-2G, and 1099-R here.

If you did not get a W-2, see page 12.

Enclose but do not attach any payment. Also, please use Form 1040-V.

12 ... 50,000,000,000

22 Add the amounts in the far right column for lines 7 through 21. This is your total income ... 50,000,000,000

Adjusted Gross Income

If line 32 is under $29,290 (under $9,770 if a child did not live with you), see EIC inst. on page 21.

I'm planning on still kicking at 128 years old and living on Mars!

Some of you may aspire to make more money. The question is how much more? Five hundred? Ten thousand? Fifty thousand? One million? And by when are you committed to making more money? Six months? One year? Five years? Making sure your goal is measurable brings an entirely new level of clarity and focus.

It is important to know what your life will look like when you are living your dreams. For example, three people may dream of being successful artists, yet all three may have a completely different picture of what that looks like in their life. One may see living her dream by painting every weekend and having occasional shows at local coffeehouses. Another person may see herself exhibiting at the New York Museum of Modern Art and annually earning $200,000 from the sale of her artwork. The third sees himself teaching art at a university. We have signs everywhere to let us know we are on the right path and have arrived at the right destination. Wouldn't it be helpful to have signs that let you know you're having the design of your life?

A Design-A-Life sets your mind at ease and your body in motion. Taking action keeps you learning. It generates valuable information about what works and what does not. This type of information you can't get any other way.

Immediate Actions with Your Future Scrapbook

Simple action can be very powerful. Start right away by taking the following actions - they produce results!

1. Periodically read your Future Scrapbook cover to cover.

2. Frame your favorite dreamalities and hang them where they are visible to others.

Immediate Actions:

1. Periodically read your Future Scrapbook cover to cover.

2. Frame your favorite dreamalities and hang them where they are visible to others.

3. Display your Future Scrapbook where others can see it.

4. Keep a copy of your Future Scrapbook with you and share it with everyone!

---

3. Display your Future Scrapbook where others can see it.

4. Keep a copy of your Future Scrapbook with you and share it with everyone!

Read through Your Future Scrapbook

Frequently flipping through your Future Scrapbook reminds you of the life you designed and rekindles the initial emotional connection. This practice can propel you into action when you are not living your life inspired by your future.

Frame Your Favorites

The Future Scrapbook was created to be seen! Having a way to share your aspirations, your future, with other people is part of the Future Scrapbook's magic. Frame your favorite dreamalities and hang them in an area such as your office where people can see them. People might think you're "famous" and it then becomes a great opportunity to share about your future.

Share, Share, Share

If you take no other action, share your Future Scrapbook with others! Carry a copy of your Future Scrapbook with you in your briefcase or in your car. You will be surprised by the number of opportunities that pop up for you to share it during your day. It is also great inspirational reading when you are at lunch or enjoying quiet time. I suggest making a list of people with whom you want to share your Future Scrapbook. Take out your day planner or calendar right now and schedule a time to call them.

"When you dream alone, with your eyes shut, asleep, the dream is an illusion. But when we dream together, sharing the same dream, awake and with our eyes wide open, then that dream becomes reality!"

Source Unknown

Sharing Reveals Unlimited Resources

Why such an emphasis on sharing the Future Scrapbook? When shared, the Future Scrapbook becomes a powerful tool for revealing new resources. When you share your dreams, people see you and relate to you in a new way. The conversation shifts from being about what you did last weekend to what your dreams are for the future. Common interests and common futures are uncovered and new connections are created. You will be amazed by all the people you already know who can contribute to your future.

Resources are often available in people that we already know, but these resources go untapped because we aren't used to having conversations about our dreams. For example, my wife recently shared with our neighbor that she is considering auditioning for a commercial. As it turned out, our neighbor formerly owned a talent agency and knew several contacts and resources in the industry. If their conversations had only focused on the weather or the lawn, this connection never would have happened.

As a result of sharing my Future Scrapbook with friends and colleagues, I have identified literally hundreds of new resources to fulfill my future. My Future Scrapbook includes me singing in a coffee shop. Since I created that future for myself, I have actively sought out people to practice with and I have been shocked at how many of my friends play instruments. Also, many people know about my aspiration to qualify for the Senior PGA tour. As a result, several people have told me about opportunities to meet PGA players and point me toward golfers who can help me to improve. Without my Future Scrapbook, these resources probably would not have developed because my friends wouldn't have known all the things in store for my future.

By publicly declaring that you'll do what it takes to achieve your deepest and truest desires, you will find it more difficult to stray from your path when frustration or challenge sets in.

Sharing your Future Scrapbook means your friends can ask, "Hey, what's happening with that project you told me about?" It is a powerful support structure that contributes significantly to having the design of your life.

If you dream of completing a marathon and one of your actions in your Design-A-Life is to run every morning at 6 a.m., aren't your friends likely to ask you how your marathon preparation is going? When your alarm goes off at 5:45 a.m., will you be as tempted to turn it off and go back to sleep knowing you'll have to admit to your friends that you didn't run? If you were meeting a running partner, would you just not show up? That's the temptation if nobody knows about your plan but you. The Future Scrapbook becomes even more powerful when you develop partnerships and teams of people to support you having the design of your life.

By publicly declaring that you'll do what it takes to achieve your deepest and truest desires, you will find it more difficult to stray from your path when frustration or challenge sets in. During a trip several weeks ago, my wife and I were discussing which car we wanted to buy next year. At first I was talking about cars that would be nice, but then we remembered that my Future Scrapbook declared I'd be driving a Mercedes by then. Sure, I considered selling out on my Future Scrapbook. (I hope it is comforting to know this happens to the author as well), but the power of having a support person busted me! Jennifer knew I had a particular car in mind, and she wasn't willing to let me settle for less than my dream.

Create Your Design-A-Life

Each of your Future Scrapbook dreamalities is a contract, evidence that your dream exists in the world. Your Design-A-

"Maybe we are
less than our dreams,
but that less
would make us more
than some Gods
would dream of."

Sister Corita Kent

Life answers the question "How did I get here?" It is also a tool to measure whether you are on course.

Examine the important stepping stones as you move toward your accomplishments. This will have a dramatic impact on how you approach future projects. If possible, do this exercise with a tape recorder or a friend who can write down your story.

1. First, pretend you have been asked to tell the story of how you accomplished your dream. However, you will tell the story as if it were the day after you accomplished it.

2. Start your tape recorder or have a friend ready with pencil and paper. Put yourself in the future with the accomplishment achieved. Look back to share where you were and describe the important stepping stones you landed on along the way.

3. Document your story as you tell it. Be as thorough as you choose - but realize you do not need to know all the details, only the critical stepping-stones.

For example, I aspire to be President of the United States. For many people with that aspiration, their past would probably include several positions in public office. However, my stepping stones are much different. They involve having leadership responsibilities in the business world, along with several volunteer civic leadership positions in my community. This aspiration, along with the story I created, resulted in me being one of the youngest people in a leadership position with my state Certified Public Accountant organization. I also was selected to be president of a non-profit organization shortly after moving to California. I doubt that I would have become this involved in my community had I not created being the President in my Future Scrapbook. I may or

Design-A-Life Template

I. This Design-A-Life is aligned with what Future Scrapbook dreamality?

_____

II. What measurable results will I produce?

_____

III. How will I reward myself for producing these results?

_____

IV. Who will I communicate with when I am stuck and not in action?

_____

V. What are my stepping stones?

1. _____

2. _____

3. _____

4. _____

VI. What actions will I take immediately?

_____

_____

_____

_____

_____

_____

may not become President of the Unites States, but that future powerfully impacts my life today!

In your Design-A-Life, you will set specific dates to reach each stepping stone. Within your Design-A-Life, develop a structure for staying in action when the going gets tough. A great way to stay in action is to create a support network. Your support team could include friends, colleagues, a personal coach or your significant other. It is important these people be positive and encouraging for you.

Here is an example of a Design-A-Life I created for writing this book:

I. This Design-A-Life is aligned with what Future Scrapbook dreamality? - *November 18, 2008, Fortunate Magazine, Prestigious Ernst & Young Entrepreneur of the Year*

II. What measurable results will I produce? - *The completed manuscript of The Future Scrapbook, Having the Design of Your Life, will be sent to the printer by September 7, 1999.*

III. How will I reward myself for producing these results? - *I will take my wife out to dinner and enjoy a seven-course meal and a great bottle of wine.*

IV. Who will I communicate with when I am stuck and not in action? - *My Future Scrapbook team and my coach.*

Develop a structure for staying in action when the going gets tough. A great way to stay in action is to create a support network. Your support team could include friends, colleagues, a personal coach or your significant other.

V. What are my stepping stones?

September 7, 1999 - *I have put the file with the completed manuscript in the mail to be delivered to the printer.*

August 9, 1999 - *I have received edited manuscripts from at least five reviewers.*

July 18, 1999 - *I have mailed at least eight manuscripts to people who have agreed to review my manuscript.*

July 11, 1999 - *The manuscript has been delivered to the editor for a final review before being mailed to the reviewers.*

June 15, 1999 - *The drafts of chapters 6,7 and 8 have been e-mailed to the editor for review.*

May 15, 1999 - *The drafts of chapters 3,4 and 5 have been e-mailed to the editor for review.*

April 23, 1999 - *The drafts of chapters 1 and 2 have been e-mailed to the editor for review.*

VI. What actions will I take immediately?

1. *I will schedule time in my calendar to call the writing team and arrange a meeting to communicate the Design-A-Life I created. I will request that they commit with me to the results.*

2. *I will create the outline for my book, <u>The Future Scrapbook-Having the Design of Your Life</u>.*

It is important that your
Design-A-Life contain
both actions and results.
So often we focus on the
results and avoid the
actions that will ultimately
produce the results.

It is important that your Design-A-Life contain both actions and results. So often we focus on the results and avoid the actions that will ultimately produce the results.

Believe in Yourself

As you begin taking actions outlined in your Design-A-Life, the mindset with which you approach this process is important. You suspended your doubts in writing your dreams, so continue believing in yourself as you take action toward your dreamalities. Act as if success is certain. Be willing to throw your hat over the fence without knowing how you'll get your body to follow.

Continually find out where you are and what you've accomplished. By all means, reward yourself for stepping stones well done. We often don't realize how far we have come because we're so caught up in the process of achieving. Allow yourself to celebrate your successes, small and large. It makes life so much more fun!

It is important to include celebration in your Design-A-Life. For example, in my game of writing this book, I included a seven-course meal with my wife to celebrate the completion of the manuscript. Without putting that in place, I can count on myself not to celebrate and acknowledge my accomplishment. I remember distinctly when I found out I passed the CPA exam on my first attempt. I called my parents and told them the good news, but that was the extent of my celebration. I studied for six months and burned many midnight candles, yet I didn't reward myself. I now know that if I include the reward as part of the Design-A-Life, I can count on myself to do it. In addition, you will be much more likely to follow through with your reward

"Try not.
Do or do not.
There is no try."

Yoda to Luke Skywalker in
The Empire Strikes Back

when you've invited guests. I promise you my wife will not let me forget my celebration of a seven-course meal!

What to Do When You Get Stopped

Now that you have your Design-A-Life and have begun to take action, what do you do when you get stopped? Talk with another person. Share where you are stopped. This helps you to get your concerns out of your head and free your capacity to be effective again.

Often it is your critical inner-voice stopping you. Remember, the critical inner-voice wakes up when you change your course and take positive action. That is why it is crucial to develop a plan to stay on course when the critical inner-voice starts to chatter. Frequent reality checks and support from friends are great ways to help you bypass this inner chatter. Look back at your Design-A-Life. Is regular communication with supportive people included?

Life won't always go according to your Design-A-Life. When your life moves at a greater velocity, your failures occur at greater velocity. Sometimes we need to trust that our disappointments are really opportunities in disguise. Like that plane, it is possible to be off course much of the time and still achieve our goals. For many of us, what we learn in life is the result of what we discovered by not doing it quite right the first time.

Take one small action towards one of your dreams. Now step out of the way. You don't have to struggle or force your dreamalities into existence. Stay in action and stay in communication, then watch the miracles happen before your eyes.

Live the Design of Your Life

CHAPTER 8

"All people of action are dreamers."

James G. Huneker

Now that you have created a compelling future and are sharing it with others, you should begin to notice a new level of vitality and effectiveness in your life. Expect unimaginable opportunities and resources to flow to you and move you rapidly toward your goals. Expect incredible, positive changes within yourself. Sometimes you may not even recognize yourself as you take bold actions that you normally wouldn't have taken. All this is part of having the design of your life!

By taking action, you continue to gain clarity about your dreams and passion pushers. You become more tuned into yourself and what you truly desire. Limiting beliefs loosen their hold on you. Areas in your life where you once operated out of a limiting belief or out of what you "should do" no longer fit. Your clear vision leads you to take actions consistent with your self-designed future.

As you become more aware of your power, you will be amazed by how much is possible. In some areas of your life, you may find that you have not dreamed big enough. Very likely, you'll have more ideas for your Future Scrapbook or outgrow some of your dreams. All this is part of the process.

Update Your Future Scrapbook

View the Future Scrapbook as a living document that changes over time, not something to complete. As you grow, your Future Scrapbook will evolve as well. Update it whenever you want. You reserve the right to change, remove or add to whatever you create.

Children's Education

August, 2007

Former Vice President Al Gore presents Nicholas and Jennifer Hall with the Humanitarian Award for their work on childrens' education.

Another original Future Scrapbook dreamility.

Face it: Yesterday's dream may not light you up today. You may no longer feel passionate when you read one of your Future Scrapbook dreamalities. These are clear signals it is time to change the story and create one that inspires and excites you. Feeling excited is critical - relating to a dream at an emotional level creates the motivation that drives it into existence.

You may have based some dreams on linear thinking, a gradual step-by-step progress, instead of quantum leaps. You may find yourself accomplishing goals earlier than planned. If so, shift your dreams and timeline accordingly.

Over time, your passion pushers may shift. Perhaps connection has become more important than adventure at a time when your Future Scrapbook shows you sailing a yacht halfway around the world. You find yourself wanting to nurture an intimate relationship or have children, so the thought of visiting foreign ports pales in comparison to the adventure of raising a child. Or do you want to have both and take your children with you on your vessel? You may want to express your passion pushers in a different way, or incorporate them with other dreamalities. Remember: There are infinite ways to express the same passion pusher. You never need to sacrifice one for the sake of another.

Being who we truly are enables us to let go of what we think we "should" be doing; we can also let go of our concerns about what people may think. You may realize that a dream you put into your Future Scrapbook is not close to your heart. Perhaps the goal was something you thought you "should do" or something that you did to please someone else - your parents or spouse, for example. Maybe you received a degree in a certain field and felt obligated to follow through with a similar career.

July 22, 2001

Dear Mom and Dad,

We can't wait for you to visit next week. You're going to love the guest room. You'll feel like you're in your own apartment with the bathroom, sitting room and kitchenette all in one area. We are so glad you're coming for two weeks. Jenn and I are looking forward to getting away for the weekend, although I'm sure we will miss Graham terribly. We're looking forward to Sally's visit next month and know she'll love the guest room, too!

We are certainly enjoying the new house. The yard is great. It is nice to have grass and trees again and enough lawn to need a lawnmower! We think the contemporary style with a bit of privacy suits us well. Building was an adventure, but worth it. Mom, you're going to love the kitchen. It is chrome and granite with lots of toys for cooking. We love our artist room. It is filled with light and is a great place to sing, paint, play music and meditate. We also have a great room for reading and relaxing. I think it is Jenn's favorite room. It has lots of pillows with rich and vibrant colors. Our master bath has a hot tub with enough room for two and a fireplace like I talked about in my perfect day.

Jenn is certainly enjoying being a stay-at-home Mom. She has a relaxing walk to the downtown area that has a great coffee shop and Italian restaurant. What else do we need? Jenn also has all the shopping she could need within a twenty minute drive and there is a great grocery store where I can get any cheese I can imagine. We are enjoying our country club membership. Our golf games are getting better and Jenn is back playing tennis again.

Future Scrapbook Enterprises is all moved in to their new digs. It is great having the office five minutes away. I think the location is working out well for everyone. I have a few speaking engagements this week, and our startup is going to close another round of financing in a few weeks.

It has been helpful having a housekeeper. I'm able to spend more time with Jenn and Graham, and I always make it home for dinner. We're having our first house-warming party in a few weeks. Graham's room is getting painted next week. I hope he likes it! We're looking forward to taking Graham on his first airplane trip in September.

We can't wait to see you. We are going to have so much fun! We really appreciate all of your help.

Love,

Nick and Jennifer

As a side note, the day Jennifer and I sat down to write this letter, we were also perusing through the Sunday paper and our horoscope (we're both Libras) read, "Change your life with something you write." Coincidence?

If you find yourself stuck or feeling uncomfortable about changing your Future Scrapbook, look to see if you are listening to a limiting belief. The Future Scrapbook isn't something you use to measure how accurately you can predict the future. Not only are airplanes off course ninety-percent of the time, they don't always depart or arrive on time either! But just because they aren't on time doesn't mean they don't keep flying!

Remain open to where new resources and ideas may lead. Remember that you are the creator of your dreams - you are the one who created them in the first place - so you are free to change them as you wish. When you do change your dreams, be sure to share them with those around you. Keep your world informed about how your life is taking shape and growing.

Before you give up a dream, ask yourself if it is the critical inner-voice or limiting belief disguised as an outgrown dream. The critical inner-voice is smart, so it is always best to double check before you budge from something that once inspired you. But if, in fact, it is time to move on, don't let those same critical inner-voices and limiting beliefs talk you into clutching a dream just because it appears in your scrapbook. This is a process about growth and excitement, not "I should" and "I have to."

Use the Process of the Future Scrapbook Every Day

At any time, you can put yourself at a future event and create concrete evidence for its success. For tomorrow's staff meeting, write a memo from your boss thanking you for a great presentation. While planning a fund-raising event, write a letter addressed to all the participants thanking them for their generous contributions. You don't necessarily need to put these

Teen Holds Party of STAR Proportions!

August 14, 2000

In the year of the new millennium fourteen year old Kasi K. of San Bruno, California held a party today of enormous caliber. Such well-known stars as Pierce Brosnan, Bruce Willis and Liam Neeson arrived at her house for a "Barbecue to Black Tie Party." Many other people showed up this afternoon for what must be the party of the year.

Barbecue ribs, deviled eggs, foods and drinks of all sorts were displayed in a wonderful array of color and style for the guests and hosts. Not only were stars there, but family and friends attended the party as well.

This is an enormous accomplishment for someone of such a young age, and most definitely deserving of recognition.

"What I want to show people with this is to reach for your dreams. No matter how far a reach it seems, go for it! You can accomplish anything you want! Just be unstoppable. This was a dream of mine for a long time, so I aimed for the moon. If I missed, I would at least catch a falling star." said Kasi earlier today.

"This has got to be the most gratifying thing I have ever done! I love it! When people grow up, they start to let 'reality' hold them back. I just worked through it. Don't let anyone tell you what you can and can't do with your life. Trust your gut. I couldn't have done it though without the support of my friends and family. I really want to thank them for all of their hard work."

Kasi is a high school freshman and lives in San Bruno, CA.

dreamalities into your scrapbook or share them with others, but they can effectively escort you to a powerful state of mind.

Your Future Scrapbook Calls You to Be Passionate Right Now!

The Future Scrapbook was designed to create a passionate life right now! What matters most is that your dreamalities bring richness to your life today.

In my Future Scrapbook, I qualify for the Senior PGA tour in 2020. I may discover another sport or hobby and decide to put my energy into that instead of golf. That isn't important. Creating this dream was about what it gives my golf game now. I have it in my schedule to play at least once each week. When I play, I focus differently and pay more attention to the details.

Imagine yourself in conversations with important people and earning prestigious awards. See how these visions influence the way you approach projects today. Whether you actually talk to the people or win the awards is secondary. The life it provides is the reward.

Expect the Unimaginable

What are you expecting today? Are you looking for a miracle or worrying about getting stuck in traffic? I strongly believe that what you look for is what you see. Look for the unimaginable. Expect miracles. Be prepared for your dreams to happen sooner than you expected. Begin to imagine all the synchronistic events and quantum leaps that will bring your dreams into play.

The dreamalities in my Future Scrapbook are becoming realities much more quickly than I ever would have imagined. I live in

"Dreams come true: without that possibility, nature would not incite us to have them."

John Updike

California years before I planned. This book has been completed faster than I (and many in the publishing world) thought possible. The magic came from sharing my dreams. Other people called me to be even bigger than I imagined. When you share your Future Scrapbook, don't be surprised when others see bigger dreams for you. And don't be surprised when they want to contribute to making those dreams happen. That is the power of sharing your future - you can count on it.

By playing for a future that requires stretching yourself in bold new ways, your journey will bring you to magnificent places that you never imagined possible. The Future Scrapbook is your life - a journey of a future created by design. May you have the design of your life.

This book would not have been a reality had it not been for the many resources I have in my life. All the resources listed here have contributed to my life in many ways. I encourage you to open your heart and mind to what they offer.

de Mello, Anthony. - Awareness, The Perils and Opportunities of Reality. New York, New York: Doubleday. *The title says it all. The book speaks to the opportunity that awareness provides to us in our lives.*

Gerber, Michael. - The E-Myth. HarperBusiness. *Provides great structures for how to approach your business and your life.*

Hill, Napolean. - Think and Grow Rich. Ballantine Books. *The first book for many entrepreneurs. It is still very powerful today.*

Landmark Education Corporation. - The Landmark Forum. www.landmark-education.com *The most impactful experience of my life.*

Robbins, Anthony. - Awaken the Giant Within. New York, New York. Simon & Schuster. *Packed full of great exercises and practices to develop your potential.*

If you have comments, thoughts or ideas about this book
I would love to hear from you. Write to me at:

Nicholas Hall
P.O Box 21107
Castro Valley, CA 94546

I can also be reached by e-mail at nick@futurescrapbook.com

THE FUTURE SCRAPBOOK TEMPLATE AND MASTHEAD CD-ROM

We have available on CD-ROM a compilation of templates and mastheads, many like the ones you saw in this book, to make it even easier to create your own Future Scrapbook. You can order the CD-ROM by:

Going to our web site, www.futurescrapbook.com. At our web site you can review some of the templates and mastheads available and download a few examples for free. You can also order by completing the form on the following page.

VISIT OUR WEB SITE

To find out more about The Future Scrapbook and the community that is being created, please go to www.futurescrapbook.com. Our web site is constantly growing and evolving and we would love to hear from you. You can join our e-mail list to receive inspiring dreamalities from people just like you. Ultimately, our vision is to create communities of people around the world who come together based upon common futures. We know that this is a step in the right direction for making our world a better place for everyone.

THE FUTURE SCRAPBOOK WORKSHOPS

The Future Scrapbook is available for your company or organization as a workshop or seminar. We have experienced facilitators and speakers around the country who can tailor the workshop to meet your needs. For inquiries or more information:

Call 1-888-665-4472

or send an e-mail to workshops@futurescrapbook.com

Nick is the inventor of the Future Scrapbook. He is also President of the Silicon Valley Association of Software Entrepreneurs. In 1998, he was the youngest recipient of the Cincinnati Business Courier's Top 40 Under the Age of 40 award for outstanding leadership. He has been an active leader with the Ohio Society of CPAs, and in 1997 was one of the youngest participants in the national CPA vision project. Nick founded three companies and started his career at Price Waterhouse.

He is designing a future he loves, which includes winning Ernst & Young's Entrepreneur of the Year Award, playing Daddy Warbucks in Annie, having four children, qualifying for the Senior PGA Tour, becoming President of the United States and celebrating his 50th wedding anniversary. Nick lives in Castro Valley, California with his wife, Jennifer.

THE FUTURE SCRAPBOOK

Call **800-852-4980** or fax your order to **707-838-2220**

Name: _____

Company: _____

Address: _____

City, State, Zip: _____

Phone: _____

Fax: _____

Email: _____

Credit Card Payments Only

☐ Visa   ☐ Mastercard   ☐ American Express   ☐ Discover

_ _ _ _ _ _ _ _ _ _ _ _ _ _ _ _ _   Exp _ _ / _ _

_____
Signatature

Quantity	Price	Total
	$14.95 / Book	
	$12.95 / CD-ROM	
California residents add 8.25% sales tax.		
Add $4.00 S&H for the first item and $1.00 for additional item		
In U.S. dollars.	**Total Amount Due**	

For payments by check, please make payable to:

RD Whitney & Co.
PO Box 1158
Newark,CA 94560